LEARNING ABOUT RELIGION

6 The King of the Jews

by **Alan Robinson**

illustrated by Derek Collard

SCHOFIELD & SIMS LTD
HUDDERSFIELD

0 7217 3026 4

First printed 1979

Printed in England by Henry Garnett & Co. Ltd.
Rotherham and London

Contents

Acknowledgements

The author and the publishers wish to thank the following for permission to use copyright material. Middle East Archive: pages 9, 12 and 22.

The Romans in Judaea

Just before the time of Jesus, a powerful people called the Romans captured Palestine and ruled over it. The Roman Empire stretched from Britain to North Africa and from Spain to Syria. The Romans came from Italy where the chief city was Rome.

The Roman army had many thousands of men. A single legion contained as many as six thousand soldiers. Some of these were not Roman by birth. In fact, almost every land conquered by the Romans provided men for the army. But Jews were not able to join the Roman army because they did not believe in the Roman gods.

For many years no other army was able to defeat the Romans because Roman soldiers were so well trained. As well as spears and swords, they had larger weapons which were used to attack towns.

A Roman prefect, or governor, ruled in Judaea, which is the part of Palestine around Jerusalem. There, as elsewhere, the Romans built forts and cities. They also built straight roads with paving stones, so that the army could move quickly from one place to another.

Most of the Roman Empire was on the shores of the Mediterranean Sea. It was much quicker to sail from Rome to Judaea than it was to travel by land. But sailing was only safe in the summer months.

The Romans were good engineers. They brought water from long distances to their towns, guiding the water along specially built channels. They even had lavatories with running water, and drains which carried the dirty water away. Roman people liked to keep themselves clean, and they built public baths where people could wash themselves.

The Romans liked entertainment. Huge, open-air theatres were built. Chariot races took place in these theatres and gladiators fought each other. Sometimes they fought wild animals.

Rich Romans enjoyed parties. Usually feasts were held in the evenings. The guests would lie on couches near the dinner-table and slaves would bring the different dishes of meat and fruit. No one used a knife or fork, but spoons were sometimes used. After dinner, musicians and dancers entertained the guests.

Something to do

1. Answer these questions.
   Why was the Roman army seldom defeated?
   Who ruled over Judaea?
   What were Roman roads like?
   What was the quickest way of travelling from Rome to Judaea?
   In what ways were the Romans good engineers?
   What entertainments did the Romans like?
2. From a reference book, find out the names of some of the Roman gods. Write a sentence about each god.
3. Imagine you were a Roman child. Describe an exciting chariot race which you have just seen.

The Land where Jesus lived

Apart from the plains near the coast of the Mediterranean Sea, much of Palestine is hilly and rocky. Further inland, there is a valley which runs the whole length of the country. In this valley are the Sea of Galilee, the River Jordan, and the Dead Sea. In summer the weather is very warm and dry, but in winter it can sometimes be cold enough for snow.

In the first century A.D. some rich Jews lived much as the Romans did. They lived in villas and some wore Roman-style dress. But many rich Jews still wore a skull cap on the head and a prayer shawl on the shoulders.

The villas were usually of stone or mud bricks. They had flat roofs and very few windows with no glass. Inside, many of them had just one large room. At one end was a platform where the family slept and where clothes and household things were stored. On the lower level the children played, the grown-ups worked and the animals were allowed to wander about.

Jerusalem was the largest city. There was a huge temple which had been restored by King Herod. Gentiles, such as the Romans, were not allowed to enter the temple. In the main hall stood an altar and a seven-branched candlestick. There was also a little room called the Holy of Holies. Outside, there were three courtyards – one for priests, one for men who were not priests, and one for women.

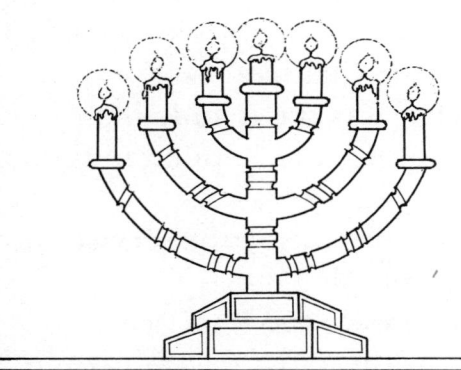

There were other buildings for worship in Jerusalem and in almost every village. These were called synagogues. Jews did not make sacrifices in the synagogues because only the temple could be used for sacrifices. After the temple was destroyed by the Romans in 70 A.D. the synagogues became the only places for Jewish worship. The people who worshipped there used to say prayers, sing psalms and listen to readings from the sacred books or scrolls.

Many scribes would be seen in the streets of Jerusalem. These were Jewish men who spent their time learning and copying the sacred scrolls. Some of them were called Pharisees and they were very strict. Every day they had to keep hundreds of laws in addition to those written in the scrolls. Especially, they had to keep themselves separate from non-Jewish people as far as possible.

Many priests would also be seen. There was a high priest who was head of the Jewish Council of Seventy, which was called the Sanhedrin. The Council was the Jewish parliament, but the Romans were the real rulers of the land. The priests, helped by the Levites (people from the tribe of Levi), organised the services in the temple.

Another important town was Jericho, which was near the River Jordan. It was often called the City of Palm Trees. Tiberias was a city beside the Sea of Galilee. Herod had built the city and named it after a Roman emperor. Most of the other towns, such as Nazareth and Bethlehem, were small and unimportant. They had street markets and the country people came there on their donkeys to do their shopping. Most Jews did not live in towns. Many had small farms where they grew fruit and grain. They would also have a few sheep and goats. Jesus of Nazareth spent most of his life among such poor country people.

Something to do

1. Answer these questions.
   What was the interior of a Jewish villa like?
   What was the temple like?
   What used to happen in the synagogues?
   Who organised the services in the temple?
   Who were the Pharisees?
   How did most Jewish people live?
2. On a map of the Holy Land, try to find these places: Jerusalem, Jericho, Nazareth, Bethlehem, the River Jordan, the Dead Sea, the Sea of Galilee.
3. Using reference books, look for some information about the Dead Sea and the Dead Sea Scrolls. Write a paragraph about each.

Jesus as a Boy

At Christmas time everyone hears the story of how Jesus Christ was born. You know already that Mary was the mother of Jesus and that he was born in a stable in Bethlehem. You will also remember that Joseph the carpenter was Mary's husband and that the Holy Family lived in Nazareth. When Christmas comes each year, Christians re-tell the story of the birth of Jesus.

Mary was very glad when she learned she was going to have a baby. The Christian Bible tells us that Mary sang a song to show how happy she was. This song is called "The Magnificat". Here is part of it:

"Tell out, my soul, the
greatness of the Lord,
rejoice, rejoice, my spirit, in
God my saviour;
so tenderly has he looked
upon his servant,
humble as she is.
For, from this day forth,
all generations will count me
blessed,
so wonderfully has he dealt
with me,
the Lord, the Mighty One."

A view of Nazareth today.

9

We know only one story about Jesus as a boy. The family used to go to Jerusalem every year for the Passover Feast. One year, when Jesus was twelve, the family travelled to Jerusalem as usual. After the feast Mary and Joseph joined all the other people from Nazareth for the journey home. They did not have Jesus with them but thought he was with friends somewhere in the crowd. After a time they realised Jesus was not with friends and they returned to Jerusalem to look for him.

After three days they found Jesus in the temple talking to the teachers. He was listening to them, asking questions and answering questions they asked him. The teachers were amazed at the answers Jesus gave. Mary said to him, "Why have you done this? We have been searching for you all over the city and we have been very worried."

Jesus replied, "You should not have been worried. You should have known that I would be in the house of my heavenly Father."

Something to do

1. Answer these questions.
   What is the name of the song which Mary sang?
   Why did the family travel to Jerusalem?
   What happened on the way home?
   What did Joseph and Mary do?
   Why were the teachers impressed with Jesus?
   How did Jesus explain his absence?
2. Pretend you were either Mary or Joseph. Write the story about how you thought Jesus was lost.
3. Write a poem or song to give thanks to God for something which has given you pleasure.

The Baptism of Jesus

There was once a prophet called John. Like many of the prophets, he lived in the desert near the River Jordan. He was dressed in a tunic of animal skin and he fastened this with a leather belt. He was a wild-looking man with long hair and an untidy beard. There was little food in the desert but he managed to survive by eating wild honey and some insects called locusts.

People used to go out into the desert to hear John speaking. He told people that God would forgive them all the things they had done wrong if they were truly sorry. He said, "Come and be washed clean in the River Jordan. Come and be baptised. Repent, and God will forgive your sins."

People walked into the river and John the Baptist poured

The place where John baptised Jesus in the River Jordan.

water over their heads.

One day John said, "God is sending a greater messenger than I; a mighty one whose sandals I am not worthy to unfasten."

Some time later, Jesus, who was now grown up, came to the River Jordan to be baptised by John. John knew immediately that Jesus was the mighty one sent by God and he said to Jesus, "You should be baptising me."

But Jesus said, "No. You must baptise me."

So Jesus walked into the water and was baptised by John. When Jesus came out of the water he heard God's voice speaking to him. The voice said, "You are my son whom I love. I am pleased with you."

Jesus knew that the spirit of God was with him.

Something to do

1. Answer these questions.
   What did John the Baptist look like?
   How did he survive in the desert?
   What did John say people should do?
   How did John baptise people?
   What did Jesus and John say to each other when they met?
   What did God say to Jesus?

2. If you have been to a christening (or baptism) describe what happened.

3. Read the story of the birth of John the Baptist, which you will find is written in St. Luke's Gospel, Chapter 1, verses 57-80. Then tell the story in your own words.

Jesus and his Disciples

When Jesus began to teach the Jewish people, he did not teach them in the synagogues but instead went round the countryside. Often, great crowds followed him. But twelve people were special followers of Jesus and they were with him nearly all the time. They were his disciples. A disciple is a pupil who is also a friend. Jewish teachers usually had a small group of disciples.

The disciples of Jesus were very ordinary men. Some were fishermen. One was a tax-collector. Another was a politician. Eleven of these men are now famous as saints, and Christians name their churches after them. The one who did not become a saint was Judas, who had sold Jesus to his enemies.

Here are the names of the twelve disciples:
Simon Peter
James
John
Andrew
Philip
Bartholomew
Matthew
Thomas
James (the son of Alphaeus)
Thaddaeus
Simon
Judas Iscariot
Jesus asked these men to follow him and they gave up their jobs without hesitation. The first four men Jesus called were two sets of brothers who were fishermen. Jesus was walking along the shore of the Sea of Galilee. Simon (later called Peter)

13

and his brother Andrew were in their boat, casting nets into the water. Jesus said to them, "Follow me and I will make you fishers of men."

Immediately the brothers left their nets and followed him.

Jesus went on a little further. James and John, two brothers, were sitting in their boat mending the nets. Jesus called to them and they followed. They left their father, Zebedee, to look after the boat with the help of hired men.

Something to do

1. Answer these questions.
   Where did Jesus teach?
   What is a disciple?
   Why did Judas Iscariot not become a saint?
   Which of the disciples were fishermen?
   What did Jesus ask the brothers to do?
   Who was left to look after the boat?
2. Make a list of Christian churches in your area. Put a star beside each church named after one of the eleven disciples.
3. Choose one of the disciples. Find some information about him in a reference book. Write a paragraph about him.

Jesus the Teacher

Jesus was a great teacher. Many of the things he said and the stories he told are in the part of the Christian Bible called the New Testament. Four writers have written about Jesus in the books we call the Gospels. They are the Gospels of St. Matthew, St. Mark, St. Luke and St. John.

Jesus often used to teach on a hill beside the Sea of Galilee. Many of the things Jesus said are written down in a part of St. Matthew's book called the Sermon on the Mount. The best-known part is where Jesus told people how to say their prayers.

He said, "Pray like this:
Our Father who art in heaven,
Hallowed be thy name.
Thy Kingdom come.
Thy will be done
On earth, as it is in heaven.
Give us this day our daily bread,
And forgive us our trespasses,
As we forgive those who trespass against us;
And lead us not into temptation,
But deliver us from evil:
For thine is the kingdom, the power and the glory,
For ever and ever.   Amen."

This is known as the Lord's Prayer because Jesus himself told it to us.

Some of the Jewish scribes did not like Jesus because he made them look foolish. He told simple stories to show people how to be good. But the scribes wanted people to listen to them, not to Jesus. One day some scribes tried to catch Jesus out. They asked him which was the most important of all the Jewish laws, hoping he would give a foolish answer.

Jesus said, "You shall love the Lord your God with all your heart, and with all your soul, and with all your mind. This is the great and first commandment. And the second is like it. You shall love your neighbour as yourself."

The scribes were astonished at this answer. They would never have thought of saying that.

Something to do

1. Answer these questions.
   Where are the stories about Jesus to be found?
   Where did Jesus often preach?
   Why did some of the Jewish scribes dislike Jesus?
   What question did the scribes ask Jesus?
   What two laws did Jesus say were most important?
   What did the scribes think about Jesus's answer?

2. Find the Lord's Prayer in Matthew's Gospel, Chapter 6, verses 9-13. What do the next two verses (verses 14-15) say?

3. Make up a prayer of your own. Ask your teacher if you can make a class-book of prayers.

How Jesus helped a Little Girl

One day Jesus was talking to a crowd beside the Sea of Galilee. A man called Jairus pushed through the crowd. He wanted to speak to Jesus about his sick daughter.

When Jesus saw Jairus he smiled kindly and asked what he wanted.

Jairus said, "My daughter is dying. Will you please come and lay your hands upon her that she may be made well?"

Jesus agreed to go to Jairus's house. Many of the crowd followed. Before they arrived a servant came from the house with the message that the girl was dead. The servant said, "There is no need to trouble the Master further."

Jesus said to Jairus, "Do not be afraid. I am still going to your house."

Jesus sent the crowd away and took with him only his three closest disciples, Peter, James and John. When they reached the house they found a small crowd in the courtyard. Many were weeping. Jesus said, "Why are you weeping? The child is not dead. She is sleeping."

The crowd laughed scornfully at these words. Only the child's parents, and Jesus and the three disciples, were allowed inside. They walked into the house, which was a large building, because Jairus was an important person. He was a leader in the synagogue.

When they reached the little girl's room they found her lying perfectly still and looking very pale. Jesus took her hand and said to her, "Little girl, stand up."

Immediately she stood up and walked. Jesus told her parents to give her something to eat. Before he left he said, "Do not tell other people what has happened."

Something to do

1. Answer these questions.
   Why did Jairus want to speak to Jesus?
   What message did the servant give?
   What did Jesus say to Jairus?
   Who was in the courtyard of the house?
   Who went into the house?
   What did Jesus ask the parents not to do?
2. Pretend there were newspapers in the time of Jesus. Write a short newspaper article about Jairus's daughter.
3. Write about a time when you were ill and how you were made well again.

The Storm on the Lake

Jesus and his disciples often went sailing on the Sea of Galilee. It was easy to obtain a boat because four of the disciples were fishermen.

One day Jesus was feeling very tired. He had been talking to crowds of people for many hours. So when evening came he and his disciples set off in a boat. It was a lovely evening. The sky was blue and the lake was calm. Jesus was sleeping on a cushion in the stern of the boat. The disciples were talking quietly so as not to waken him.

Suddenly a wind began to rise. In a few minutes there was a gale blowing. The sky was black and huge waves were splashing over into the boat. It was a long way to the shore and the boat was filling with water. The disciples were afraid, but Jesus slept on peacefully.

At last one of the disciples woke Jesus up and said to him, "Master, we are all going to drown. Don't you care?"

Jesus spoke to the wind and the sea, saying, "Peace! Be still!"

Immediately the wind stopped

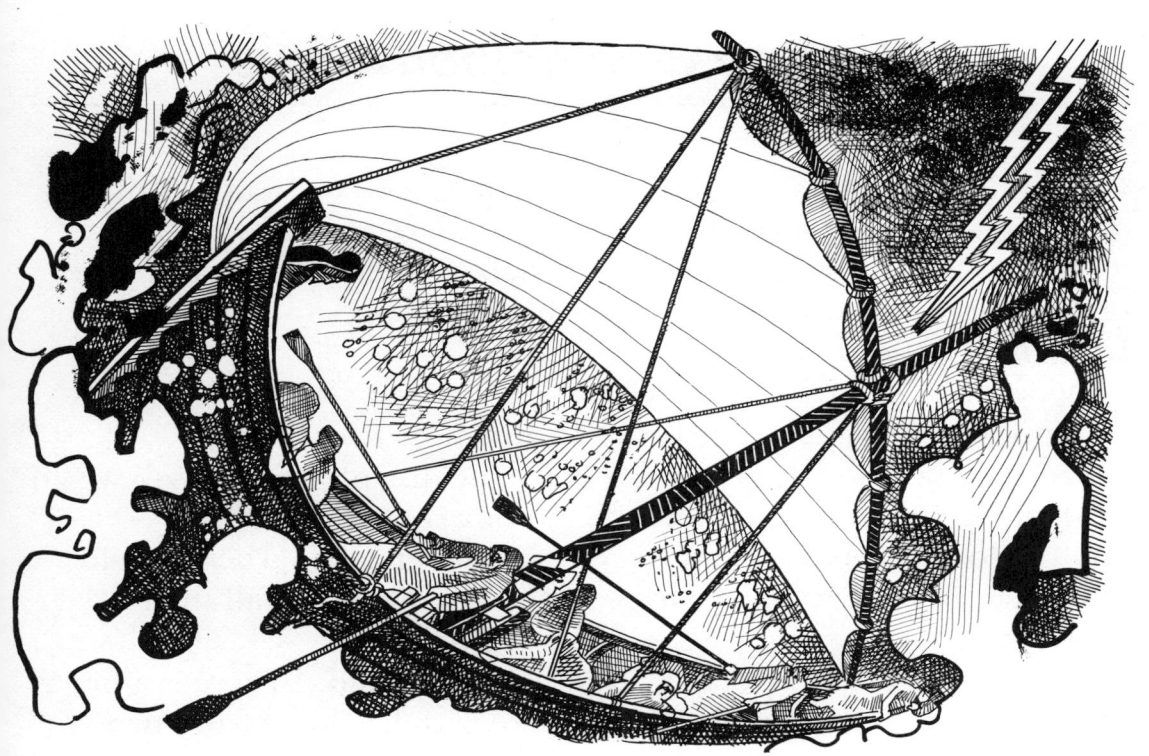

blowing and the water was calm
again. Jesus said to the disciples,
"Why were you afraid? You
should know that when I am
with you there is no need to
fear."

Something to do

1. Answer these questions.
   Why could Jesus and his
   disciples easily obtain a boat?
   Why was Jesus tired?
   What was the weather like
   when they set off in the boat?
   When the storm came, how
   did the disciples feel?
   How did Jesus deal with the
   situation?
   What did he say to his disciples
   afterwards?
2. What do you think the
   disciples would talk about
   while Jesus slept? Write a
   conversation in which Peter,
   James and John take part.
3. Write a modern adventure
   story about a miraculous
   escape in a storm at sea.

The Boy who helped Jesus

On another day Jesus and his disciples set off in a boat. They wanted to find a lonely place because of the crowds. Even Jesus liked to be alone sometimes.

Many people watched the boat leave. They said to one another, "Let's walk round by the shore. We'll follow the boat and find out where Jesus is going. Perhaps he will talk to us again."

Some of the crowd managed to arrive before the boat. They were waiting when Jesus landed and he felt sorry for them. So, even though he was tired, he began to tell some more stories.

When it was late in the day the disciples said to Jesus, "This is a quiet place and it is very late. Shall we send the crowds to the nearby villages to find something to eat?"

Jesus said, "You give them something to eat."

One disciple said, "Shall we go to buy some bread?"

Another said, "There would not be enough for all these people."

Andrew said, "There is a boy here with five loaves and two fishes. He is willing to share them but they will not go far."

Jesus asked the crowd to sit down. It happened to be a grassy place and everyone was

comfortable. Altogether there were about five thousand people in the crowd.

Jesus then took the loaves and fishes in his hands. He said a prayer to thank God for the food. He broke the bread and fishes into pieces and passed them round. Everyone had enough to eat and there was a lot of food left over. Twelve baskets were filled with the pieces.

Something to do

1. Answer these questions.
   Why did Jesus sometimes like to be alone?
   Why did the crowd follow by the shore?
   What did the disciples suggest the crowd should do?
   What did the boy bring?
   What did Jesus say before the meal?
   How did Jesus feed the crowd?
2. Write an account of the story of the loaves and fishes, beginning with these words: "I was one of the crowd that day, listening to Jesus by the lake."
3. There are many hungry people in the world. Can you suggest ways in which your class could help them?

The Good Samaritan

A scribe once asked Jesus what he should do to please God.

Jesus answered, "Love God and love your neighbour."

The man said, "Do you mean my next door neighbour?"

Jesus replied, "Anyone in need is your neighbour and you should help him."

Then Jesus told this story.

"A man was travelling along the desert road from Jerusalem to Jericho. On the way some robbers attacked him. They took his money and beat him, leaving him half dead. Some time later a priest passed by. When he saw the injured man he pretended not to see him and crossed to the other side of the road. A little later an assistant priest came along. He, too, crossed the road and pretended not to see the man. Then a third person came. He was from Samaria. The Samaritans and the

The Inn of the Good Samaritan on the Jericho Road.

Jews disliked one another. But this Samaritan saw the wounded man and felt sorry for him. He dressed his wounds and put him on his donkey. There was an inn nearby, so he took the man there. He then gave the innkeeper some money and asked him to take care of the man."

Jesus turned to the scribe and asked, "Which of these three men was the good neighbour to the man who was robbed?"

The scribe replied, "The one who helped him."

Jesus said, "Go, then, and do the same."

Something to do.

1. Answer these questions.
   What did Jesus mean by a neighbour?
   On which road was the man in the story travelling?
   What happened to him on the journey?
   What did the priest and the assistant priest do?
   What did the Samaritan do?
   Who is the good neighbour in the story?
2. Describe what you would do if you found someone lying injured outside your house.
3. Ask your teacher to tell you about the work of the "Samaritans" today. Make a list of some other organisations which exist to help people.

The Father who forgave his Son

A man had two sons. The younger one wanted to leave home. His father gave him his share of what money there was and a few days later the son set out for a far country. In a very short time he had spent all his money and was a poor man.

He decided to take a job. It was not a very exciting one. He had to look after some pigs in a field and see that they were fed. One day, while watching the pigs, he said to himself, "Even my father's servants are better fed than I am. I will go back to my father and ask him to forgive me."

He made the journey home. The day he arrived his father saw him in the distance and ran to meet him. Clasping his son in his arms he welcomed him.

The younger son said, "Father, I have done wrong. I am not a good son."

His father smiled and said to a servant, "Bring new clothes for my son, and shoes. Bring a ring for his finger. Kill one of the calves for a feast. I thought my son was dead, but he is alive."

So they had a magnificent feast.

Meanwhile, the elder son was working in a field at some

distance from the house. When he heard the music he wondered what had happened. A servant explained that his brother had returned. The elder son was annoyed at this and refused to go to the feast, even though his father pleaded with him.

He said to his father, "I have stayed at home and worked for you all this time. But you did not give me a feast."

His father said kindly, "My son, you are always with me. And I am grateful. But I thought your brother was dead and he is alive. Surely you can see that it was right to celebrate his home-coming."

Something to do

1. Answer these questions.
   What happened to the younger son when he left home?
   Why was he unhappy?
   Why did he return home?
   What did the father do when the younger son came home?
   Where was the elder son?
   What did the elder son say to his father?
2. Write a story about a boy or a girl who does something wrong and is sorry afterwards.
3. Make up a story about the older brother who stayed at home.

Jesus on the Mountain

One day Jesus said to his disciples, "Who am I?"

Peter answered, "Master, you are the Messiah, God's son."

Jesus said, "You must not tell people about this. Keep it to yourselves."

A few days later Jesus took with him Peter, James and John and they walked to the top of a high mountain. At the top Jesus said, "Wait here."

Then he walked a little way from the three disciples. As the three waited there, Jesus was changed in front of their eyes. His clothes glistened and shone, whiter than any person could wash them. Two men seemed to be talking to Jesus. The disciples thought they must be Moses and Elijah.

Peter suggested that they should make three stone tables,

one for Jesus, one for Moses and one for Elijah. While they were doing that, a cloud of mist came down on to the mountain. A voice came out of the cloud, saying, "This is my son whom I love. Listen to him."

When the disciples looked round, the two men had disappeared and Jesus was standing alone.

On the way down the mountain, Jesus asked the three disciples not to tell anyone what they had seen.

Something to do

1. Answer these questions.
   Whom did Peter say Jesus was?
   Who climbed the mountain with Jesus?
   How was Jesus changed while on the mountain?
   According to the disciples, who were the other two men?
   What did the disciples do?
   Whose voice spoke from the mist?
2. What can you remember about Moses and Elijah? Write a paragraph about each of them.
3. Write a poem or story about being lost in the mist on a mountain.

Jesus arrives in Jerusalem

Jesus and his disciples travelled to Jerusalem for the Passover Feast. On the last part of the journey Jesus rode on a donkey. The people knew that he was coming and lined the streets, shouting and cheering. They even spread palm leaves across the road like a carpet of welcome. They called, "Hosanna! Blessed is he who comes in the name of the Lord!"

When Jesus reached Jerusalem he went into the temple. He was very angry to see the courtyard full of traders who were selling animals and birds for sacrifices. He overturned the tables of the money-changers and chased them out of the temple, saying, "You have made the house of God into a den of thieves!"

The priests and scribes did not like this. They were also jealous because Jesus was popular, so they planned to kill him.

When the time came for the feast of the Passover, Jesus and his disciples gathered in an upstairs room in the city. It was evening and they all sat round the table, Jesus and his twelve friends.

As they were eating, Jesus took bread and blessed it. He broke it into pieces and gave it to the disciples, saying, "Take and eat; this is my body."

The he took a cup of wine, and when he had blessed it he passed the cup to them, and they each drank from it. And he said to them, "This is my blood, which is poured out for many."

Before the supper was over, one of the disciples, Judas, slipped out of the room. He was on his way to meet the priests and scribes, because he was going to betray Jesus to them for money.

The supper which Jesus had with his disciples is called the Last Supper. Today, during the Holy Communion service in church, Christians eat bread and drink wine to remind them of that supper.

Something to do

1. Answer these questions.
   How did Jesus travel into Jerusalem?
   How did the people welcome him?
   What did Jesus do in the temple?
   Why did he do this?
   Where was the Last Supper held?
   Who planned to betray Jesus?
2. Can you think of three reasons why the priests and scribes wanted to kill Jesus?
3. In a reference book, find some information about the Christian service of Holy Communion. Write a paragraph about it.

Good Friday and Easter Sunday

Jesus was in the Garden of Gethsemane with all his disciples except Judas. While in the garden Jesus prayed to his Father in heaven for strength, because he knew what was going to happen to him.

After a time, Judas came along with a crowd of priests and scribes. Some of them were carrying weapons. Judas kissed Jesus. This was the signal to the priests, who immediately arrested Jesus.

He was taken before the High Priest who said to him, "Are you the son of God, the Messiah?"

Jesus answered, "I am.'

The High Priest said, "You deserve to die for saying such a thing."

The priests and scribes could not execute Jesus. Only the Romans could do that. So Jesus was taken to the Prefect, Pontius Pilate. After asking Jesus some questions, Pilate wanted to set him free, but the crowd outside shouted, "Crucify him! Crucify him!"

Pilate decided to let the people have their way. Jesus was given to the soldiers. They dressed him in a purple cloak and put a crown of thorns on his head. Then they mocked him, saying, "Greetings, King of the Jews."

On the way to the execution a man called Simon helped Jesus to carry his cross because it was so heavy. Two robbers were crucified at the same time, one on each side of Jesus. The soldiers gambled to see who would have the clothes belonging to Jesus. They also put a notice on the cross, reading, "The King of the Jews".

Before Jesus died he said, "Father, forgive them because they do not know what they are doing."

When Jesus was dead, he was buried in a tomb with a huge stone rolled across the entrance. The tomb belonged to a man called Joseph of Arimathea.

That happened on a Friday, later called Good Friday. On the Sunday afterwards, three women went to the tomb, carrying spices so that they could anoint Jesus's body. They found the tomb empty. The body of Jesus had gone.

The women ran to tell the disciples what had happened. They all wondered, "Can Jesus really be alive?"

They found that Jesus *was* alive, because he appeared to them several times. That Sunday became known as Easter Sunday, which is a special day for Christians.

Something to do

1. Answer these questions.
   Where did the arrest of Jesus take place?
   How did Judas give a sign to the priests?
   Why did the High Priest not execute Jesus?
   What did the soldiers do to Jesus?
   Who helped Jesus to carry his cross?
   Where was Jesus buried?
2. Write a story entitled, "I was the centurion at the Crucifixion".
3. Make a model depicting a scene from the Easter story.

The next booklet in this series is called *The First Christians*. It tells the story of the church founded by the disciples of Jesus.

Notes for the Teacher

Background

The Romans dominated the Mediterranean area during the lifetime of Jesus of Nazareth and it seems right to examine the Roman background.

The Roman general Pompey made Judaea a Roman province in the year 63 B.C. From that date, the country was ruled by various puppet kings, including Herod I who reigned from 37-4 B.C. Jesus was born during the reign of Herod I (see Matthew 2, 1). This means that he was probably born in 4 B.C. or a little before that date. This, of course, is a subject for debate among scholars.

After Herod the Great's death, the kingdom was divided among his three sons. (A) Archelaus ruled as Ethnarch in Judaea from 4 B.C.-6 A.D. From then until 41 A.D. a series of Procurators ruled (Pontius Pilate, 26-36 A.D.). From 41-44 A.D. King Agrippa ruled over the Judaean area. He was brother to the notorious Herodias, wife of Herod Antipas. (B) Herod Antipas ruled as Tetrarch in Galilee and Southern Transjordania from 4 B.C.-39 A.D. (C) Philip ruled as Tetrarch in Northern Transjordania from 4 B.C.-34 A.D.

Under the Procurators of Judaea, the Jewish Council, the Sanhedrin, was allowed some political power. The High Priest was the most powerful person after the Procurator. He was, of course, a religious leader, but also led the domestic government. In addition to the High Priest there were seventy members of the Council.

The two main parties of scribes were the Pharisees and the Sadducees. The Pharisees were the party of the common people while the Sadducees were generally of aristocratic descent.

A useful book for New Testament background is *Everyday Life in New Testament Times* by A. C. Bouquet.

It is difficult to do justice to the life and teaching of Jesus in a single booklet. However, it is assumed that the children will hear many other stories from the Gospels in school assemblies and especially at Christmas and Easter.

A simple version of Jesus's life, death and resurrection is presented, including some examples of his work and teaching. An attempt has been made to follow the Bible stories quite closely, but using language which is within the comprehension of 9-10 year-old children.

Detailed Notes

Page 5. Roman citizenship could be purchased. St. Paul was proud of the fact that he had been born a Roman citizen. Of course, citizenship was not restricted to inhabitants of Rome.

Prefect or governor – properly "procurator".

Emperor – the first Roman emperor was Octavian, later called Augustus (30 B.C.-14 A.D.). Tiberius ruled from 14-37 A.D.

Page 6. Prayer shawl – called "the great tallith".

Page 7. Herod's temple – see *Everyday Life in New Testament Times* by A. C. Bouquet, page 288, where a detailed plan is given.

Holy of Holies – as far as is known, the Ark of the Covenant, which had been kept in Solomon's temple was destroyed in 587 B.C. with the first temple. There were no windows in the Holy of Holies and, when Pompey captured Jerusalem in 63 B.C., he was surprised to find that the sanctuary was an empty room.

The Pharisees believed in the oral law which was a large body of laws added to the written law. These were later recorded in the Talmud. The Sadducees did not accept the oral law.

Page 9. Mary's Song or the Magnificat is similar to Hannah's Song about the birth of Samuel. Whether Hannah and Mary wrote these songs is doubtful. The children do not have to understand every word of the poem in order to appreciate it. Only St. Luke gives us the Magnificat.

Page 10. The teachers would be priests and scribes, learned in the Hebrew scriptures.

Page 11. Locusts – it is part of jungle survival technique to eat insects.

Baptism was not a new custom. Jews had practised ritual washing for many generations. However, John gave a new dimension to the rite which survives in Christian practice. Some Christian groups insist on total immersion in water.

Page 12. Baptism of Jesus – the traditional simile about the dove has been omitted because it leads to confusion between fact and symbol.

Page 13. The politician was Simon the Zealot, Zealots being activists against Roman rule.

The names of the apostles – there are alternatives for some of the names.

Page 15. The Sermon on the Mount is to be found in Matthew 5-7. Many scholars think it unlikely that Matthew was the author of the Gospel which bears his name. name.

Page 16. The two laws given by Jesus are both in the Old Testament. He was quoting them, not inventing them. By choosing these two laws as essential, he cut through the legal strata of a thousand years to regain the true spirit of the law.

Page 17. In the middle of the story about Jairus, Mark's Gospel inserts another story about Jesus healing a sick woman. This has been omitted.

The crowd outside the house was probably made up of professional mourners.

Peter, James and John. At certain critical times Jesus chose to take these three disciples into his confidence.

Jairus was an elder in the synagogue.

Page 20. The feeding of the five thousand – various attempts have been made to rationalise this and other miracles. For example, some people believe this is an example of a miracle of sharing. The boy shared his food and so everyone else who had food shared it out. However, not all miracles can be explained away and it is advisable to leave the interpretation open.

Page 21. The Good Samaritan – it would be appropriate here to talk to the children about the work of the "Samaritans" today.

The people of Samaria were disliked by the people of Judaea who thought they were not true Israelites. This makes the story more pointed. A hated Samaritan, and not the priest, nor the Levite, was the good neighbour.

Page 23. The use of the word prodigal would be unhelpful in this story.

Page 24. The story of the Transfiguration is necessary for an understanding of the Messiahship of Jesus. The story can be accepted by the children at a simple level without the complication of abstract interpretations.

Page 26. This account of the institution of the Last Supper adheres closely to the account in Mark's Gospel.